AMERICA

THE BATTLE FOR IRAQ:

CBS NEWS **SIMON & SCHUSTER**

NEW YORK LONDON TORONTO SYDNEY SINGAPORE

AT WAR

A VIEW FROM THE FRONTLINES

DAN RATHER AND THE
REPORTERS OF CBS NEWS

SIMON & SCHUSTER
Rockefeller Center
1230 Avenue of the Americas
New York, NY 10020

For information about special discounts for bulk purchases,
please contact Simon & Schuster Special Sales:
1-800-456-6798 or business@simonandschuster.com

Photo Credits:
Page 73: photo copyright Damir Sagojl/Reuters
Page 114: photo copyright Cheryl Diaz Meyer/*Dallas Morning News*
All other photos copyright AP/Wide World Photos

Edited by Susan Ellingwood and Teresa Tritch
Maps created by Philip Mirante, David Rosen, and Jared Thaler

Designed by Joel Avirom and Jason Snyder
Design assistant: Meghan Day Healey

Manufactured in the United States of America

10 9 8 7 6 5 4 3 2 1

Library of Congress Cataloging-in-Publication Data is available.
ISBN 0-7432-5786-3

CONTENTS

INTRODUCTION

There are two lessons that we as a people learn anew every time we take up arms: Each war is different from those that came before. And every war is the same.

There was much that made the war in Iraq unique, from the weapons with which it was fought to the way it was covered to the circumstances that led to those first air strikes on Baghdad on the night of March 19, 2003. This war was quick: U.S.-led forces required only three weeks to seize the capital city of a foreign power and less than a month to put an end to major combat. But this war also bore an extended preamble, an unusually long period marked by faltering diplomacy and a creeping sense of inevitability. And toward the end of that time before the fighting began, there came a reminder of this war's terrible kinship with every war that has ever been.

CBS News correspondent Jim Axelrod was embedded with elements of the Third Infantry Division in northern Kuwait as they prepared for the thrust into Iraq that would bring them to Saddam Hussein's abandoned palace. He asked a private, a young man girding himself physically, emotionally, and spiritually for battle, if he was afraid that war would not be what he expected it to be.

"I'm worried," the enlisted man replied, "that it's going to be exactly what I expect."

Nations all have their reasons for fighting wars, and some observers have opined that this war was as elaborately justified as any in memory. President George W. Bush and his cabinet laid out their case before the United Nations, before Congress, before the American people, and before the world: Saddam Hussein harbored weapons of mass destruction; he was in league with terrorists; he was a tyrant, a threat to his neighbors, and a destabilizing force in a region where stability is so badly needed.

History, it has been said, is an argument without end, and it is history that will be the judge of the second Gulf War and the justifications behind it. But as we debate, we might also remember that those we called on to fight this war offered no arguments once the battle was joined. When the order came down, it fell to American and allied soldiers, Marines, sailors, and fliers to put reasons aside and perform their duties. As a nation, we Americans understand this now in a way that we perhaps failed to during the Vietnam era; it is an understanding that lies behind the words "I support our troops"–words shared by this war's most vehement advocates and opponents alike.

By the time the Third Infantry Division traversed the sand berm that separates Kuwait from Iraq, a majority of Americans stood behind

President Bush's decision to go to war. But there was also a sizable minority of antiwar sentiment. Many in this country echoed an international chorus of dissent over the war's preemptive nature, its lack of U.N. backing, and the potential risks of new conflict in such a volatile part of the world.

Maybe it was in part because of this divide in our national discourse that Americans of all ideological persuasions focused so closely on the heroic efforts of our fighting men and women. Because of the embed program, which put journalists among our armed forces as they fought, we were afforded an unprecedented chance to see these special people up close, in real time, as they went about their work. It was an instructive, often harrowing view into a world of death and danger, of superb professionalism and awe-inspiring endurance. I don't know anyone who watched and who, regardless of his or her feelings about the war itself, came away without a true sense of pride and admiration for these Americans in uniform. I know the same is true of the journalists who had the opportunity to share their world.

This war saw what can genuinely be called revolutionary innovations in its planning, in its weaponry, and on the battlefield. When it comes to armed combat, we have seen the future and this is it. Digital technology adapted by the U.S. military to new weapons engendered what may be the most important battlefield innovations since the advent of the machine gun. The great accuracy and highly concentrated destructive power of these weapons have changed military thinking about strategy and tactics worldwide, and will continue to do so for years to come.

We are witness to an era during which air power is in the ascendancy, while the value of tanks, artillery, and massed ground armies declines. Speed, flexibility, maneuverability, precision, and dominance of the space above the battlefield were the hallmarks of this technological blitzkrieg, and now all nations that wish to exercise military power, and those that aspire to, must digest these realities and adapt.

In recognizing and accepting this, though, there is a danger—that we will overemphasize and become mesmerized by the technology, by the new equipment of war, while failing to give the human factor its due. While the importance of air and space power grows, no one should underestimate the continued need for disciplined and well-equipped infantry. No war, including this one, has ever been won without boots on the ground. In the end, to win, an armed force must *walk* in and take over. And it should not be forgotten that wars, as ever, exact a terrible toll in flesh and blood.

War is primitive at its core. This latest, most modern of conflicts echoed with many of the same agonies, complications, and triumphs that rang from the windswept plains of Troy and, in this case, the riverbanks of Babylon. The first true war of the digital age was fought on the planet's oldest battlefield, a place where armies and cultures have clashed since the dawn of civilization. Old and new commingled in this second Gulf War in ways that told us both how far we have come and how little, regrettably, we have changed.

The people who walk the ground, drive the tanks, fly the planes, and steer the ships—combatants and civilians—usually do so far from home. In the dark and lonely times of danger, they experience fear of dying with a depth that is impossible for anyone who has not experienced it firsthand to fully comprehend. To paraphrase the Korean War reporting of the late Eric Sevareid, what makes the fear of death so deep is the fear of dying with no one at home knowing how it was, how it really was, and what he or she was trying to do—the intolerable fear of death in anonymity.

Wars, even short ones, are savage. Their purpose is to kill people and break things. Abraham Lincoln, author of a war we now regard as noble and necessary, perhaps put it best when he said: "There is no honorable way to kill, no gentle way to destroy." Because wars are so violent and brutal, there is an understandable but regrettable human tendency to elide the tough truths they contain. This is particularly true among victors. And it is most particularly true in the wake of a quick victory, such as that gained by America and its allies in Iraq.

As of this writing and from the time the fighting started, some 170 Americans, dozens of allies, and untold thousands of Iraqis—combatants and civilians—have been killed. As wars go, this casualty toll is generally considered "low," so it is easier to gloss over the casualties of this war than in most. And easier to forget what war is, which is real blood, mud and sand, real maiming and killing, real screams of the wounded and moans of the dying.

We saw much but we did not see it all. No matter how compelling their pictures or accounts, reporters cannot hope to translate the full experience of war for those at home. In the heat and glare of battle, there is not always ample time for reflection on just what it all means, how the images that rush past us join the broader, less readily perceived stream of world events. Wartime journalism inevitably confronts a paradox: Television news can provide unrivaled immediacy but can be less successful at supplying the sort of context and depth that only the written word can convey.

This book and DVD have been put together with this very much in mind. Between these covers and on this disc are the reports of CBS correspondents, with emphasis on those who chronicled frontline battlefield experiences. Journalists are fond of saying that they provide "a first draft of history," and indeed, in many ways they do. But by definition most first drafts are incomplete and—let's face it—sometimes misleading or otherwise wrong. In compiling a narrative from a variety of first drafts of this war's history, we have no illusions. This is not, and cannot be, anything close to a definitive history of the war in Iraq. At best, it is a collection of written and visual snapshots that future historians may want to peruse as source material. And one that you may want to read, watch, consider, and reflect upon as a multifaceted view of a war that riveted the world's attention in the spring of 2003.

Years ago, the famed Irish journalist and essayist Robert Lynd wrote: "The belief in the possibility of a short, decisive war appears to be one of the most ancient and dangerous of human illusions." In Iraq, in the early years of the twenty-first century, the awesome military power of the United States would seem to have given the lie to the "short" part of this wisdom. U.S.-led forces executed a daring battle plan with brilliance and courage—and in record time.

But as this remembrance of those twenty-eight days of fighting goes to press, the war cannot yet be termed decisive. In the near term, Iraqis and their American occupiers still confront the deprivations wreaked on that country by decades of tyranny and relentless conflict. Looming humanitarian crises, exacerbated by endemic looting, threaten to transform Iraqi relief at Saddam's ouster into resentment over the confusion and want that have followed the toppling of that first statue in Baghdad.

Looking further down the road, crucial issues relating to the building of democratic institutions in Iraq will need to be resolved with diplomatic skill and aplomb commensurate with that brought to bear in the military effort. The region once called Mesopotamia is a minefield of deep-seated resentments between Sunni and Shiite Muslims, Arabs, and Kurds; passions long pent within the power of Saddam's iron fist have now been freed with unknowable results. The war has been won, but that in and of itself is no guarantee of victory for the uneasy peace.

Few endeavors in the human realm can match war for its unpredictability, and the immediate effects of military triumph in the heart of the Middle East are just now revealing themselves to us. It will take many months and years before we and those who come after us can reckon the full and far-reaching consequences—for the United States, for Iraq, and for the world—with anything approaching finality or consensus. When we consider the degree to which we still live in the shadow of World War II, itself brought about by the first world war, we must realize that we, ourselves, may not live to see whether or not the United States has, in this war, made the illusion of a "short, decisive war" into a new reality.

For the present, though, we can offer what we saw and what we know of the war as it raged—as the United States by force of arms brought a new Iraq into an uncertain world.

DAN RATHER
CBS NEWS
MAY 2003

AMERICA AT WAR

CHRONOLOGY OF A WAR

TIME RUNS OUT

JANUARY 29, 2002

In his State of the Union speech, President George W. Bush claims Iraq is part of an "axis of evil."

SEPTEMBER 12, 2002

At the United Nations, President Bush challenges the General Assembly to confront Iraq and says that the United States will act alone if necessary.

NOVEMBER 8, 2002

The U.N. Security Council unanimously adopts resolution 1441 threatening "serious consequences" if Iraq fails to comply with new weapons inspections.

NOVEMBER 27, 2002

The United Nations resumes weapons inspections in Iraq.

DECEMBER 7, 2002

Iraq formally states that it has no weapons of mass destruction.

FEBRUARY 5, 2003

Secretary of State Colin Powell presents U.S. documentation of Iraqi weapons of mass destruction to the U.N. Security Council.

FEBRUARY 15, 2003

Worldwide antiwar demonstrations draw millions of protestors into the streets.

MARCH 1, 2003

Turkey denies the United States access to its bases.

MARCH 5, 2003

France, Germany, and Russia declare that they will not allow a resolution permitting military force to pass the U.N. Security Council.

MARCH 7, 2003

For the fourth time in less than three months, weapons inspector Hans Blix tells the United Nations that Iraq has not cooperated fully.

MARCH 16, 2003

President Bush meets with the leaders of Britain, Spain, and Portugal on the Azores.

MARCH 17, 2003

In a televised speech, President Bush tells Saddam Hussein to leave Iraq within forty-eight hours or face military action.

MARCH 19, 2003

War begins with air strikes on Baghdad targeting Saddam Hussein and his top aides.

MARCH 20, 2003

The ground assault begins as U.S. and British forces move into Iraq from Kuwait.

MARCH 21, 2003

Baghdad and other targets come under intense U.S. bombardment with the goal to "shock and awe" the Iraqi leadership into surrender.

Two U.S. Marines are killed in southern Iraq becoming the first reported combat casualties of the war.

COMBAT

MARCH 22, 2003

General Tommy Franks, commander of allied forces in Iraq, reports that 1,000 to 2,000 Iraqi fighters have been taken prisoner and thousands more have fled.

Grenade explosions kill one officer and injure fourteen others in an apparent fratricide attack in Kuwait.

Scattered fighting in southern Iraq presages deadlier encounters.

MARCH 23, 2003

In Nasiriya, Umm Qasr, and Basra, unexpected resistance from fedayeen and other irregular forces thwarts the U.S. attempt to bypass or quickly secure cities en route to Baghdad.

Two are taken prisoner when ground fire forces their Apache helicopter to land near Baghdad. In a separate incident, twelve U.S. soldiers are reported missing. Later, Iraqi television shows five of the missing soldiers, the two pilots, and dead bodies believed to be those of U.S. soldiers.

MARCH 24, 2003

The onset of three days of brutal sandstorms further slows the ground advance to Baghdad.

MARCH 25, 2003

Intense fighting occurs in Najaf between U.S. forces and Iraqi militia.

President Bush asks Congress for $74.7 billion to cover war-related costs through September 30.

MARCH 26, 2003

More than 1,000 U.S. troops parachute into areas controlled by Iraqi Kurds to open the war's northern front.

Civilian casualties mount with a daytime explosion in a Baghdad marketplace. Later, Iraq blames the United States, but the United States questions its culpability.

MARCH 27, 2003

Advancing toward the northern oil city of Kirkuk, Kurdish fighters under U.S. command occupy the city of Chamchamal.

MARCH 28, 2003

In northern Iraq, Kurdish troops and U.S. Special Forces destroy a base of Ansar al-Islam, a fundamentalist group with alleged ties to Al Qaeda.

British relief ship arrives in Umm Qasr with more than 200 tons of food, water, and medicine.

MARCH 29, 2003

A suicide bomber kills four U.S. soldiers at a checkpoint near Najaf.

MARCH 30, 2003

Bombs continue to pound Baghdad and the northern cities of Mosul and Kirkuk.

Civilians fleeing Basra are fired on by Iraqi militia in the city.

MARCH 31, 2003

North of Najaf, U.S. troops open fire on a van that doesn't make a required stop at a checkpoint, killing seven women and children.

APRIL 1, 2003

Prisoner of war Private First Class Jessica Lynch is rescued from an Iraqi hospital by U.S. Special Forces.

U.S. ground troops enter the "red zone," the area around Baghdad where military officials say they're most vulnerable to attack by chemical weapons.

ALL BUT WON

APRIL 2, 2003

U.S. forces defeat Iraqi forces in Karbala and Kut.

APRIL 3, 2003

U.S. Army forces begin to take control of Saddam International Airport on the outskirts of Baghdad.

The Iraqi capital is blacked out. The Pentagon denies targeting the power grid.

A pregnant woman is killed, along with three U.S. special operations troops, in an apparent suicide bombing near the Haditha Dam, northwest of Baghdad.

APRIL 4, 2003

Iraqi television shows Saddam Hussein making an appearance on the streets of Baghdad.

APRIL 5, 2003

U.S. tanks and other armored vehicles roll through Baghdad, drawing fire and killing Iraqi fighters. Civilian casualties mount as noncombatants are caught in the cross fire.

APRIL 6, 2003

Intense fighting ensues around Baghdad as U.S. forces encircle the city.

In northern Iraq, U.S. warplanes mistakenly bomb a convoy of U.S.-backed Kurdish fighters, killing at least seventeen and injuring forty-five.

APRIL 7, 2003

British troops enter Basra.

A U.S. bomber drops massive bombs on a building complex in Baghdad where intelligence sources say Saddam Hussein is meeting with his two sons and other Iraqi leaders.

APRIL 8, 2003

A U.S. tank fires on the Palestine Hotel in Baghdad, killing two journalists. U.S. missiles hit the Baghdad office of Al-Jazeera, killing one journalist.

APRIL 9, 2003

U.S. Marines pull down a statue of Saddam Hussein in central Baghdad. Excited onlookers beat the toppled statue.

APRIL 10, 2003

Looting and mayhem prevail in Baghdad and other cities, including Kirkuk, which falls to Kurdish fighters and U.S. Special Forces, and Najaf, where a prominent pro-Western cleric is murdered.

APRIL 11, 2003

Anarchy intensifies in Baghdad as homes, hospitals, shops, and government buildings are ransacked.

Looting is already under way in Mosul as Kurdish and U.S. forces enter the northern oil-rich city, Iraq's third largest.

U.S. military issues "wanted" cards for fifty-five former top Iraqi officials.

APRIL 12, 2003

Looters are reported to have stolen and destroyed at least 170,000 artifacts from Baghdad's National Museum of Antiquities.

APRIL 13, 2003

U.S. Marines advance on Tikrit, Saddam Hussein's hometown.

U.S. Marines find seven U.S. POWs north of Baghdad.

APRIL 14, 2003

U.S. Marines take control of Tikrit.

In London, Prime Minister Tony Blair claims "victory" in Iraq.

APRIL 15, 2003

In Washington, President Bush declares "the regime of Saddam Hussein is no more."

In the ancient city of Ur, former exiles, sheiks, clerics, and ethnic Kurds meet to discuss the future of Iraq.

Looting continues in Iraq's major cities.

APRIL 16, 2003

General Franks convenes his key officers in one of Saddam Hussein's Baghdad palaces, later telling reporters that "the decisive combat portion of the campaign is finished."

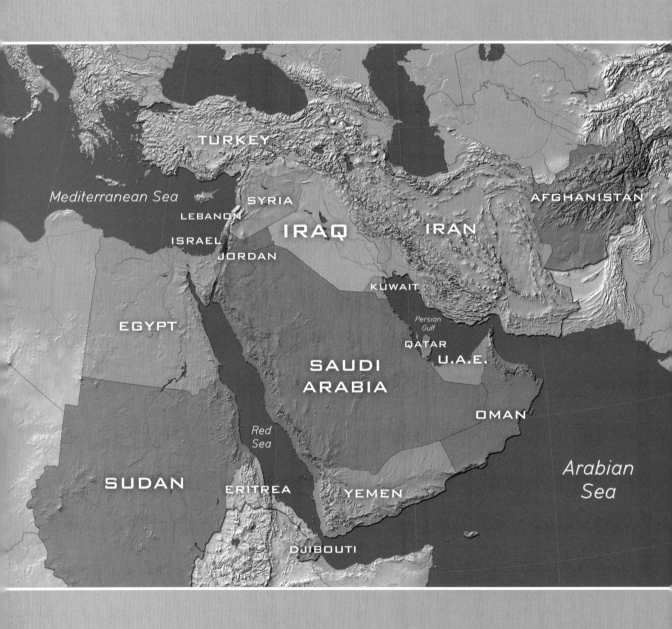

TIME

RUNSOUT

ABOVE During a presentation at the United Nations, U.S. Secretary of State Colin Powell alleges that Iraq possesses thousands of gallons of anthrax. Here, he holds up a vial that he says could contain enough of the bacteria to cause death and disruption.

LEFT Foreign ministers at the United Nations listen to U.S. Secretary of State Colin Powell's presentation on Iraq's weapons program.

THE MARCH TO WAR

To hear U.S. Secretary of State Colin Powell tell it, the Bush administration was never in a rush toward war. Powell spent seven and a half weeks negotiating Resolution 1441 line by line, word by word. By the time it was approved unanimously by the fifteen-member U.N. Security Council in November 2002, as far as Powell was concerned, everyone—including the French, the Russians, and the Germans—knew that the resolution's reference to "serious consequences" meant only one thing: either Saddam Hussein complied fully with new weapons inspections or the Bush administration would go to war with Iraq.

But the diplomatic wrangling was not over. By March 2003, Paris and Moscow's call for a second resolution authorizing force had been joined by London, Washington's staunchest ally. Public sentiment throughout Europe against a war was strong, and this made already skeptical leaders more nervous. Many Europeans thought President Bush's personal style was brash and that he was morally arrogant.

The policy disagreement boiled down to this: The Bush administration saw Saddam Hussein as a clear and present danger. Having suffered one huge attack on September 11, 2001, President Bush was unwilling to take any chances that the Iraqi dictator would allow weapons of mass destruction to fall into the hands of terrorists for use in another attack.

Led by France, much of Europe's political leadership didn't see the threat in immediate terms and refused to pledge support for a second resolution.

On the Security Council, Britain, Spain, and Bulgaria were firmly behind the United States on a second resolution. Five other members—France, Germany, Russia, China, and Syria—were firmly opposed. Washington was left looking for five of the six votes from those who were undecided: Mexico, Chile, Pakistan, Cameroon, Angola, and Guinea.

But France threatened to use its veto if Washington got the nine votes required for passage, thus escalating the policy disagreement into a political and diplomatic crisis. In many ways, the confrontation over Iraq had become a test among Security Council members of how much the United States could get away with as the world's only remaining superpower.

Faced with a possible veto, the U.S. withdrew the resolution on March 17. That evening, President Bush delivered his ultimatum speech, giving Saddam Hussein forty-eight hours to leave Iraq or face military action.

CHARLES WOLFSON
STATE DEPARTMENT REPORTER, CBS NEWS

NO TO WAR

On one weekend in February 2003, millions of antiwar protestors take to the streets in cities around the world: Barcelona, Sydney, London, Istanbul, Cairo, and New York City.

ABOVE British Prime Minister Tony Blair urges the House of Commons to support U.S. efforts in Iraq. At right is British Foreign Secretary Jack Straw.

LEFT French president Jacques Chirac (right) consults with his prime minister the day after the leaders of France, Germany, and Russia declare that they will block a new U.N. resolution authorizing military force against Iraq.

In an interview televised on February 26, 2003, Dan Rather (far left) and Saddam Hussein (far right) had the following exchange:

RATHER: Mr. President, do you expect to be attacked by an American-led invasion?

TRANSLATOR FOR SADDAM HUSSEIN: We hope that the attack will not take place. But we are bracing ourselves to meet such an attack, to face it. . . . You've been here for a few days and you've seen how the people live. They live normally. They get married. They establish relationships. They visit each other. . . . They are enjoying life in the manner that life has provided. . . . But . . . because the officials in the United States keep talking about attacking Iraq . . . they get prepared for such a possibility.

SAYING
GOOD-BYE
Troops prepare to deploy
for war with Iraq.

"THE DAY OF YOUR LIBERATION IS NEAR"

My fellow citizens, events in Iraq have now reached the final days of decision. For more than a decade, the United States and other nations have pursued patient and honorable efforts to disarm the Iraqi regime without war. That regime pledged to reveal and destroy all its weapons of mass destruction as a condition for ending the Persian Gulf war in 1991. Since then, the world has engaged in twelve years of diplomacy. We have passed more than a dozen resolutions in the United Nations Security Council. We have sent hundreds of weapons inspectors to oversee the disarmament of Iraq. Our good faith has not been returned.

The Iraqi regime has used diplomacy as a ploy to gain time and advantage. It has uniformly defied Security Council resolutions demanding full disarmament. . . . Intelligence gathered by this and other governments leaves no doubt that the Iraq regime continues to possess and conceal some of the most lethal weapons ever devised.

This regime has already used weapons of mass destruction against Iraq's neighbors and against Iraq's people. . . .

22

In an address to the nation on March 17, 2003, President George W. Bush gives Saddam Hussein forty-eight hours to leave Iraq.

The United States and other nations did nothing to deserve or invite this threat, but we will do everything to defeat it. Instead of drifting along toward tragedy, we will set a course toward safety. Before the day of horror can come, before it is too late to act, this danger will be removed.

The United States of America has the sovereign authority to use force in assuring its own national security. Recognizing the threat to our country, the United States Congress voted overwhelmingly last year to support the use of force against Iraq. America tried to work with the United Nations to address this threat because we wanted to resolve the issue peacefully. We believe in the mission of the United Nations. . . .This is not a question of authority, it is a question of will.

Last September, I went to the U.N. General Assembly and urged the nations of the world to unite and bring an end to this danger. On November 8, the Security Council unanimously passed Resolution 1441, finding Iraq in material breach of its obligations and vowing serious consequences if Iraq did not fully and immediately disarm. . . .

Yet some permanent members of the Security Council have publicly announced that they will veto any resolution that compels the disarmament of Iraq. These governments share our assessment of the danger, but not our resolve to meet it. . . .

All the decades of deceit and cruelty have now reached an end. Saddam Hussein and his sons must leave Iraq within forty-eight hours. Their refusal to do so will result in military conflict, commenced at a time of our choosing. For their own safety, all foreign nationals, including journalists and inspectors, should leave Iraq immediately.

Many Iraqis can hear me tonight in a translated radio broadcast. And I have a message for them. If we must begin a military campaign, it will be directed against the lawless men who rule your country and not against you. As our coalition takes away their power we will deliver the food and medicine you need. We will tear down the apparatus of terror. And we will help you to build a new Iraq that is prosperous and free. . . .

The day of your liberation is near. . . .

EXCERPT OF A SPEECH BY
PRESIDENT GEORGE W. BUSH
ON MARCH 17, 2003

Iraqi demonstrators in Baghdad rally in support of Saddam Hussein on March 18, 2003.

As war looms, Iraqi Kurds leave their homes in the city of Irbil in northern Iraq, hoping to find safety in mountain villages.

ON THE
FLIGHT DECK

The bombing of Iraq began on March 19, 2003, and continued through the war.

OVERLEAF Troops gather in the Kuwaiti desert.

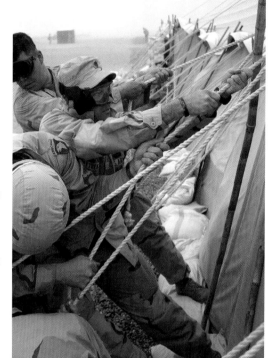

Fighting against 40 m.p.h. winds, troops struggle to stabilize a tent.

Soldiers attend a pre-operation briefing.

CH-47 Chinook helicopter crew members prepare to take flight.

Euphrates
River ▶

Baghdad

IRAN

Kut

Tigris
River ▶

Karbala

**101st
Airborne**

Numaniyah

Najaf

Marines

**3rd
Infantry**

Amarah ○

Samawah ○

**82nd
Airborne**

Nasiriyah ○

IRAQ

Basra

Umm
Qasr

KUWAIT

TOP **President George W. Bush announces that war has begun and says, "The only way to limit its duration is to apply decisive force."**

ABOVE **Saddam Hussein appears on Iraqi television several hours after the initial U.S. air strikes on Baghdad. Some experts raise questions about the tape's authenticity.**

TO THE FLIERS, SHOCK AND AWE WAS JUST ANOTHER MISSION

t was March 21 at 8:23 in the evening, Iraq time, and Baghdad was about to be blasted. The other journalists and I aboard the USS *Abraham Lincoln* in the Persian Gulf knew that something was up because the crew was ready to launch twenty-five of the ship's fighter jets, each fully loaded with bombs.

"Operation Shock and Awe" was getting under way.

But aboard the USS *Lincoln,* a different mindset was evident. Earlier in the day, when Captain Scott Swift, the deputy commander of the air wing, briefed reporters on the aircraft carrier, he refused to call the impending campaign Operation Shock and Awe. He referred to it as "just another mission." We argued: "But Donald Rumsfeld calls it Shock and Awe." He shrugged and shook his head.

Yet to my eyes, the amount of firepower on the carrier was indeed shocking and awesome. Bombs were everywhere: lying next to basketball goals in the hangar, stored in the enlisted sailors' cafeteria, and piled up in areas on the flight deck called missile farms. It was as if all available space had been taken over by 2,000-pound bombs on rollers.

As the mission began, I stood on the deck and watched the fighter jets line up, two at a time, behind three catapults that launch them from zero

37

to more than 150 miles per hour in seconds. As the jets moved into launch position, other fighters waited their turn. It looked a lot like O'Hare at rush hour, except these were long, sleek F/A-18 Hornets and F-14 Tomcats and the rounder S-3B Viking, tankers used for refueling that one of the pilots called "play school" planes because they have no sharp edges.

I also spent time with the Blue Wolves squadron in their ready room before they went out on a refueling mission. The room looked like a small movie theater, with forty or so cushioned seats in a row. Over one of the seats hangs an enormous bolt. A bolter is what pilots call a returning plane that misses the arresting wire and has to try a second time to land. The bolt is hung over the chair of the last pilot who missed, and it won't be moved until someone else bolts. This dubious distinction is a reminder to the pilots to be humble, despite the power they control.

And in fact, while some sailors have a "let's kick butt" attitude, others appear dismayed by the display of power. Watching the bombing of Baghdad on television in one of the computer learning rooms a lieutenant turned away from the set and told me, "This is too much. It looks like overkill." A few others watched silently, then turned away.

Everyone is united in joy as the planes begin to return. The flight deck crew trades high fives and pumps the air with their fists. The last of the jets that launched that night made it back just before one in the morning. By then, the USS *Constellation,* also in the Gulf, had already begun launching its jets into Iraq.

CYNTHIA BOWERS
CORRESPONDENT, CBS NEWS

INTENSIVE BOMBING

OPPOSITE AND ABOVE The U.S. begins massive "shock and awe" bombardment of Baghdad and other cities on March 21, 2003.

COMBAT

MOVING OUT

The waiting ended just after midnight in Kuwait on March 21. That's when the 10,000 vehicles and 17,000 troops of the U.S. Army's Third Infantry Division, some of whom had been in Kuwait for half a year, started crossing into Iraq. Tank after tank rolled by, and fresh-faced soldiers flashed thumbs-up from their Humvees.

I, along with my cameraman and technician, was embedded with the First Brigade Combat Team of the Third Infantry Division, 5,000 frontline soldiers operating M1 Abrams tanks, Bradley fighting vehicles, Paladin howitzers, and multiple launch rocket systems, among other weapons. The First Brigade was the first to cross the border into Iraq and remained in the lead all the way to Baghdad.

For the next thirty hours, with vehicles on each other's bumpers, the convoy would push 150 miles into Iraq. My cameraman drove for all but thirty minutes of those first thirty hours. It was grueling. Most of the driving was done at night to avoid being seen by the enemy. No headlights. No brake lights. No streetlights. Night vision goggles helped, but since they offer no depth perception, the driving required enormous concentration to avoid slamming into the vehicle in front. The worst fear was getting separated from the group.

About seventy-two hours into the northward advance, the First Brigade stopped and set up camp southeast of the Karbala Gap, a narrow strip of land that was a critical area to cross on the way to Baghdad. Unfortunately, it was also an easy place for a convoy to get snarled in a traffic jam. The Army wanted to prepare the area by killing or capturing as many Iraqi troops as possible, so that the convoy would not become sitting ducks.

While the First Brigade camped in the desert for eight days, various units targeted Iraqi positions, heading out to secure nearby towns such as Najaf and villages like Kifl.

Each night, soldiers would return with stories of skirmishes, which were usually the first combat experience for the younger soldiers. Often the resistance was persistent, but pathetic: a state-of-the-art M1 Abrams tank facing off against a run-down pickup truck with an old Soviet machine gun mounted on the back.

Were those Iraqi fighters suicidal to take on the U.S. Army? Were they brave defenders of their country's sovereignty? Were they desperate? Were their families threatened by Saddam loyalists? I couldn't tell and never got to ask them. But I know what I saw—decisive overwhelming use of sophisticated U.S. weapons against opponents using broken down Kalashnikovs and even Flintlock rifles. After a week of fighting, the First Brigade could count their casualties on one hand.

The sandstorm that swept in on March 25 slowed the pace of the advance. Even the most technologically sophisticated military was no match for nature. The weather also changed the mood of the troops. The inaction combined with the salmon-colored glow in the air invited reflection.

During the sandstorm, units kept heading out to secure territory. The roughest battle for the First Brigade was in Kifl, a small village on the banks of the Euphrates near Najaf. My crew and I visited Kifl during a break in the three-day battle. Iraqi bodies and bombed-out vehicles littered the streets. In the passenger seat of one car was nothing but a rib cage. The stores were deserted. Hanging on the wall of a barbershop was a large mural of New York City's World Trade Center set on the banks of the Euphrates surrounded by lush palm trees. It wasn't a trophy painting of the destroyed Twin Towers. It looked like it had been painted years before—a picture of paradise.

JIM AXELROD
CORRESPONDENT, CBS NEWS

GROUND ASSAULT
Coalition forces move into southern Iraq
from Kuwait: The U.K.'s Scottish armored
brigade (left) and a U.S. Marine (above).

SURRENDER
Up to 2,000 Iraqi soldiers
were taken prisoner
by the third day of the
war, according to General
Tommy Franks, commander
of allied forces in Iraq.

LEFT Unidentified Iraqi soldiers surrender to British Royal Marines in southern Iraq.

ABOVE U.S. Marines give water to an Iraqi soldier who surrendered an hour after the Marines crossed into Iraq from Kuwait.

SOLDIERS
OF THE NIGHT

t was only two days into the war when my cameraman and I were given the rare opportunity to accompany a team of U.S. Special Forces on a flight into Iraq, where they planned to disembark and take control of an airstrip. We would be heading deeper into southern Iraq than any U.S. troops had yet to venture.

We were crammed into a C-130 cargo plane in the middle of the night—two fully loaded Humvees, about a dozen troops, two journalists, and enough equipment and supplies for a week in the desert.

Often seen as mavericks, Special Forces were crucial in the opening days of the war, but so secret were their missions that most weren't disclosed until they were history. Some may never be revealed. In fact, my cameraman and I couldn't tell anyone what we saw for at least twenty-four hours. The missions depend on secrecy. Most of the soldiers go by nicknames or call signs. Many haven't had their photos taken since high school. And they all look upon publicity as a detriment to their livelihood.

As we crossed into Iraq, the plane swooped to within 250 feet of the desert, and all lights in the plane went off, to better avoid enemy detection. I could see only one soldier, uncomfortably positioned between the tire of a jeep and the plane's bare fuselage. An eerie red flashlight lit up the pages of a well-worn letter from his wife. His lips moved as he read the words silently to himself.

A tap on my shoulder by the team leader indicated we were about to land. The soldier folded his letter, slipped it inside a pocket in his armored vest, and braced for the hard, abrupt landing.

Before the plane even stopped, the jaws of the cargo doors opened. The soldier quickly gathered his gear, hoisted an enormous pack on his shoulders, and then softly patted his pocket. He disappeared with the other secret soldiers into a desert that until that night they had seen only on a map.

LEE COWAN
CORRESPONDENT, CBS NEWS

GROUND TROOPS ENGAGE

While moving through southern Iraq, U.S. and British forces
encounter Iraqi resistance.

An Iraqi casualty lies
along a road in the
Al Faw Peninsula.

n the moonlight, I could see a group of U.S. soldiers surrounding a prisoner. They were menacing, cussing, and screaming, "Did you do it? Why did you do it?" Their guns were pointed at his head. He was sprawled facedown in the desert dust, his hands bound behind his back, his legs bleeding.

But he wasn't an Iraqi soldier, he was a sergeant in the U.S. Army.

About an hour before the capture, two grenade explosions had rocked the camp of the First Brigade of the 101st Airborne Division in Kuwait, home to 4,700 soldiers. The first one, at 1:21 in the morning, jolted me awake. Ten seconds later, the second one sounded, louder and closer. I heard someone cry, "I've been hit, I've been hit!" We all lunged for our helmets and flak jackets and ran outside, where soldiers were everywhere in blurry motion.

On the other side of our complex of ten tents, half-dressed soldiers rushed out the wounded on stretchers. I couldn't get a hard look at the injured. What I saw was blood—on legs, torsos, and faces, and in some cases, what looked like a first try at triage: crude bandages and tourniquets. I walked into one of the attacked tents. I could smell cordite, and through the smoke, see a hole in the rubber floor. A major stood there, dazed. "I saw the tent flap open up," he said. "And a grenade just rolled in."

There was enough order in the chaos to account for everyone. But during the head count, Sergeant Hasan Akbar, who was with an engineering group attached to the 101st, turned up missing. Several grenades were also missing. Three had been tossed into tents where officers were living, but only two of them had detonated. Akbar was found hiding in a bunker, three more grenades tucked into his gas mask bag.

Colonel Ben Hodges was the First Brigade's commander. While the search for Akbar was on, he told me that the soldier-suspect was a convert to Islam. He seemed worried that the news might complicate the war effort at a time when the U.S. military was also trying to win a diplomatic battle with the larger Islamic world. Still, after Akbar was apprehended, Hodges accepted that my cameraman and I would release the video and the information.

The resentment toward Akbar was palpable. The consensus among soldiers I talked to was that he should have been shot on the spot. "Isn't that what they do with traitors during a war?" one soldier asked me.

MARK STRASSMANN
CORRESPONDENT, CBS NEWS

Following a shocking grenade attack by a fellow
soldier, the First Brigade, 101st Airborne Division
mourns the death of Captain Christopher Seifert.

F R I E N D   O R   F O E

Marine Corporal Mike Breslin was trained to ease off the trigger when civilians appeared in the sights of his M-16. But on Sunday morning, March 23, in the Iraqi port of Umm Qasr, Breslin and 130 other men of Fox Company found themselves pouring withering fire into a building full of people in civilian clothes.

"They're just too cowardly to wear their uniforms and stand up and fight us," the twenty-two-year-old Marylander told me after the battle.

Three days into the war's ground assault, the men of Fox Company, Second Battalion, First Marine Regiment, engaged an enemy they didn't recognize. About forty fighters from Saddam's fedayeen commandos had maneuvered to the edge of the port, driving civilian cars and trailing white flags. They took positions in a three-story building a few hundred yards from the Marines. The Americans were getting a meal-ready-to-eat for breakfast when the fedayeen started firing.

In response, the men of Fox Company sprinted toward the incoming fire. They threw themselves down along the crest of a sand berm and opened up with machine guns, mortars, and Javelin guided missiles. The firefight lasted five hours. It ended when Marine M-1 tanks lumbered toward the building and killed the last of the plainclothes fighters with a

64

half-dozen blasts from their 120-millimeter cannons. None of the Marines was wounded.

After the fighting, Captain Rick Crevier, the commanding officer of Fox Company summed up the situation in a tone that was both matter-of-fact and laced with disgust: "We've learned they don't respect white flags," he said. "So it requires us to have our head on a swivel."

In these early days of combat, the war didn't go as expected. Some towns, like Umm Qasr, were thought to be under control, only to erupt in fighting. Other towns, wrenched from Saddam's iron grip, were in free fall. On March 22, when my crew and I entered the town of Safwan near Umm Qasr, we were the only Americans there. Both American and British forces had swept through the town and left it. At the hospital, an angry crowd of townspeople showed us their dead and wounded and begged us for medicine. "We need police," one man told us. "There are bandits everywhere." Another shouted, his voice breaking, "You tell Bush, we need water, water, water!"

We did not realize it then, but the unconventional battles, lawlessness, and humanitarian crises of these early days foreshadowed what was soon to come in the far larger cities of Basra and Baghdad.

SCOTT PELLEY
CORRESPONDENT, CBS NEWS

TOP LEFT **A U.S. Army Apache helicopter was shot down south of Baghdad. The two-man crew was taken prisoner and later shown on Al-Jazeera, the Arabic satellite network.**

BOTTOM LEFT **Army soldier Shoshana Johnson was among the members of the Army's 507th Maintenance Company who were ambushed after getting lost near Nasiriya. She was taken prisoner and later shown with other U.S. captives on Iraqi television and on Al-Jazeera.**

OPPOSITE **A Marine patrols near the southern city of Nasiriya.**

INCOMING WOUNDED

At first it was a cakewalk.

By March 20, the second day of the war, the aviation brigade of the Army's Third Infantry Division had secured the airfield at Jalibah, outside Nasiriya, about forty miles from the border with Kuwait. The aviation brigade and its team of Apache helicopters had then provided air support for, among others, the First Brigade of the Third Infantry Division as it crossed a bridge over the Euphrates River on the way to Baghdad.

The Iraqi regular army soldiers in the area, poorly equipped and badly demoralized, had put up no real resistance, and were either killed in the skirmishes or fled.

So a few hours after the successful bridge crossing, the Third Infantry Division determined that the Iraqi Eleventh Army Division had been "defeated" and declared that the U.S. Army had "won the battle of Nasiriya." But in fact, the battle had not yet begun.

As the First Brigade continued on toward Baghdad, the aviation brigade stayed at Jalibah awaiting the Marines who were coming into Nasiriya behind the Army. The aviators believed the area was safe, but just in case, they set up a medical station—well, really, just a Humvee with a red cross on its side, equipped with some medical supplies and staffed by one doctor and one field medic.

On March 23, things changed. The Saddam fedayeen, Iraq's paramilitary fighters whose name means "one who sacrifices himself for a cause," had laid low as the Army passed through Nasiriya. But they hit the Marines hard.

By the afternoon, Marine assault support helicopters, or CH-46 Sea Knights, began flying into the Army's makeshift medical station with injured U.S. Marines, Iraqi fighters, and civilians who had been caught in the cross fire. One helicopter arrived carrying the lifeless bodies of about eight U.S. Marines. About three to six casualties were arriving every hour. Between helicopter landings, the overworked Army doctor and medic trained soldiers in basic medical skills—how to set up stretchers; how to keep an IV flowing; how to inject morphine.

Taking in the scene, I stood at the head of one stretcher. I couldn't properly see the Marine's face, but I could see he was missing his entire right hand; it looked as if it had been chopped off clean. He was conscious, and we were talking, trying to keep things light. A soldier walking by asked me who I was. I told him I was embedded media from CBS. The wounded Marine suddenly shot out, "CBS? Phil, is that you?" I came around and looked into the face of Marine Captain Jason Frei.

Weeks before the war had started I had spent ten days with Frei's artillery battery covering the buildup and the preparations for war. Frei, thirty-one, is a thoughtful man, and contrary to the stereotype of a Marine, he is gentle-spirited. We had gotten along great. Standing there, I remembered how pleased he'd been when I promised to e-mail his family the digital photos I had taken of him and his buddies.

I remember helping to carry Frei's stretcher to the ambulance that would take him to a Marine helicopter for the flight to a hospital in Kuwait. I remember saying, "God bless, Captain, and take care." It was all I could think of to say.

PHIL ITTNER
REPORTER AND PRODUCER, CBS NEWS

AMBUSHED

We were three days into the war and still no sign of the enemy. I was with the U.S. Marine Second Light Armored Reconnaissance Battalion on the outskirts of Nasiriya, a strategic crossing point over the Euphrates River about 200 miles south of Baghdad. "This is too easy," one Marine said to me.

But the war was about to become infinitely more difficult. The next day, on March 23, our column was waiting to move into the city when news came that eighteen from another unit had been killed and several soldiers from the 507th Army Maintenance Company had been captured in Iraqi ambushes in and around Nasiriya: Fighters from Saddam's brutal fedayeen militia had feigned surrender and then opened fire on the troops while the lightly defended 507th took a wrong turn and ran straight into Iraqi forces. "Damn" was all one Marine could say to me. Some raged against the Army, who a day earlier had proclaimed Nasiriya safe. Others simply went silent.

The commander of the Second Light Armored Reconnaissance Battalion, Lieutenant Colonel Eddie Ray, wanted to dive immediately into the fight—to take the pressure off ground troops caught in a no-man's-land between two key bridges. But his senior officers told him to wait. The reasons for this are still unclear. Vowing to show the fedayeen "how the Marines do it," he finally punched through with his unit—a full thirty-six hours later. By then, the fighting in Nasiriya had tied up the Marines' advance and generally made a mess of the U.S. battle plan.

I entered Nasiriya in a convoy the morning after Ray went in. Marines from a number of different units were fighting to hold a thin ribbon of road that ran adjacent to the militia's stronghold. Commanders kept our vehicles far enough apart that the Marines could shoot across the road, engaging the militia, as we passed by. Overhead, Cobra gunships unleashed their deadly sting. The ground shook when the heavy Abrams tanks opened up. Oily smoke roiled out of Iraqi tanks and armored transports. The air was filled with an acrid smell that will forever conjure up images that the mind would rather forget: headless bodies; civilians cut down in the cross fire; scarred prisoners. There was death in abundance.

JOHN ROBERTS
CORRESPONDENT, CBS NEWS

CROSS FIRE

A Marine doctor cradles an Iraqi girl whose mother had just been killed in fighting near Rifa.

Three days of desert sandstorms starting on March 24, 2003, slowed the advance to Baghdad and complicated the fighting.

NORTHERN FRONT

The Kurdish fighters of northern Iraq placed themselves under U.S. command to achieve the common goal of overthrowing Saddam Hussein.

"WE HAVE ALWAYS LIVED IN FEAR"

Northern Iraq is a panorama of snowcapped mountains and rolling green fields that belies its violent history. During the spring when the war took place, my crew and I often saw colorfully dressed Kurdish women planting their crops—apparently oblivious to the distant sound of artillery and aerial bombardment.

Between four and five million of the world's approximately thirty million ethnic Kurds live in northern Iraq, most of them in the "safe haven" that was established by U.S. and British forces after the first Gulf War. Their autonomy from Baghdad notwithstanding, Iraqi Kurds harbor a deep hatred of Saddam Hussein, who attacked them with poison gas in 1988 and brutally suppressed them when the United States encouraged them to revolt in 1991. But in spite of having been betrayed by the U.S. then and during a previous uprising in 1975, the Kurds willingly joined forces with Washington as the war became imminent. They even pledged to abandon their goal of establishing an independent Kurdistan—a move that would rock the region by inflaming neighboring Turkey and Iran—in favor of working with the United States to achieve a Saddam-free Iraq.

Feelings of hope ran deep, even if they were qualified. At a Kurdish checkpoint on the road to the northern oil-rich city of Kirkuk a few days before the war began, a peasant family offered us tea. Sitting in a circle on the ground outside their modest compound, they were unconcerned about being within gunshot range of Iraqi forces. "We have always lived in fear," the weather-beaten family patriarch said. "But now, Inshallah [God willing], we will soon have a better life."

The first significant battle of the northern front began on March 28, against Ansar al-Islam, a fundamentalist Islamic group with alleged ties to the terrorist Al Qaeda network. Under the command of U.S. Special Forces, the peshmerga—Kurdish guerrillas whose name means "those who face death"—ousted Ansar from strongholds on the border between Iraq and Iran. Afterward, U.S. soldiers gushed uncharacteristically about the peshmergas' courage. "To watch them fight is something to see, how fast they can do it and how fierce they are," one Special Forces officer said. Scores of peshmerga were killed. After one battle we saw a dozen bodies taken from the scene of the battle in the back of a dump truck. No one is certain how many Ansar fighters died—either shot or buried in caves blasted by air strikes—or how many escaped to Iran.

On April 11, as the combat in northern Iraq drew to an end, we finally entered Mosul, an oil center and Iraq's third largest city. It fell to Kurdish and U.S. forces with virtually no resistance from the Iraqi defenders, who had been battered by heavy air strikes. Along the highway south, hundreds of Iraqi soldiers, who had thrown away their uniforms, were walking away from the burning city. As we videotaped them, I recalled an Iraqi soldier who a few weeks earlier had waved to our camera from a pitiful bunker positioned near the road to Mosul. Was he lucky enough to be among those men trudging home? Or had he been vaporized for a cause he had to know was lost?

As the Iraqi army abandoned northern towns and cities, looters took over the streets. Arab residents of Mosul blamed Kurds for the mayhem. Clashes between the two groups intensified as Kurds from other parts of northern Iraq returned to the city from which they had been exiled during Saddam's long campaign to "Arabize" the north. In the rush to reclaim their former homes, Kurds were heedless of danger. Carloads of families raced down roads where land mines might be planted. We saw youngsters exploring bunkers where shells were stored. Civilians were shot at by hold-out Saddam loyalists or by Arabs who believed the Kurds were coming to loot their homes. It was a final irony: Northern Iraq seemed more dangerous in victory than in war.

ALLEN PIZZEY
CORRESPONDENT, CBS NEWS

HUMANITARIAN AID

ABOVE A U.S. Navy mine-detecting dolphin helped to clear the port of Umm Qasr in preparation for the arrival of the British Royal Navy's relief ship *Sir Galahad*. The ship brought food, water, and medicine for distribution to Iraqi civilians.

RIGHT A British sailor walks across a cargo of humanitarian aid in Umm Qasr.

HELP ARRIVES

**Initial distributions of aid by British
troops draw frenzied crowds near Basra.**

TRYING TO HELP

We were not the people they wanted to see: "We" were a busload of journalists; "they" were the residents of the bleak southern Iraqi border town of Safwan, where several days earlier, U.S. and British forces pushing through to Baghdad had met little resistance. We knew that trucks carrying humanitarian aid were following behind us. All they seemed to know for sure was that they'd been without food and clean water for nearly a week.

As we parked on the outskirts of town, a large crowd of people—mostly young men and children—materialized out of nowhere. I got off the bus and

Lack of clean water plagued several Iraqi cities and towns.

was surrounded by a dozen or more men wearing the traditional red-and-white kaffiyehs and chanting pro-Saddam slogans. "We will give our blood," they shouted. "We will give our lives to Saddam Hussein." I had been expecting a warm welcome, so I was disconcerted, even though I tried to tell myself that these Iraqis probably didn't want to be thought of as traitors to the regime, especially in front of our cameras.

Then five or six of the men standing around me suddenly began to grope me, putting their hands inside my blouse and in my slacks. Trying not to panic, I swatted their hands off of me, at which point they began to rifle through the backpack I had slung over my shoulder. I had resigned myself to being robbed when a loud rumbling sound behind me caused the men to pause and then leave me alone. The food trucks had arrived.

Aid workers from the Red Crescent, the Islamic equivalent of the Red Cross, barely had time to slide open the truck doors before they were pushed aside by dozens of Iraqi men who jumped aboard, frantically grabbing boxes. What I had thought would be an uplifting story about winning the hearts and minds of the Iraqi people was in reality an ugly scene of desperate men fighting anyone—even old women—for food and water. To avoid being trampled, those of us who had come to cover the story were forced to stand at the periphery.

As I was standing aside, a barefoot little girl, maybe five or six years old, shyly touched my arm with one hand, and with her other, excitedly pointed to a barrette in her hair that matched the one I was wearing.

ERIN MORIARTY
CORRESPONDENT, CBS NEWS

LEFT British soldiers of 40 Commando, Royal Marines, patrol the region after taking the Al-Faw Peninsula oil installations in southern Iraq on March 21, 2003.

ABOVE U.S. military convoys head north to Baghdad.

U.S. Army soldiers approach
an injured woman shot in cross
fire between Americans and
Iraqis on a bridge over the
Euphrates River.

U.S. Army Bradley fighting
vehicles fire on Iraqi positions
along the Euphrates River while
seizing a bridge.

SUICIDE BOMBER

An Iraqi man driving a taxi detonated a bomb, killing himself and four American soldiers near Najaf on March 29. This led to more stringent controls at checkpoints throughout Iraq.

MORE QUESTIONS THAN ANSWERS

t was late on the night of April 1, and everyone was tense. We were sweating out another night on the outskirts of Nasiriya, just south of "Ambush Alley," as the Marines called the main supply route to Baghdad. Morale among the young Marines around me couldn't have gone much lower: Eighteen soldiers had been killed in a vicious ambush the previous week. Several others had been wounded in smaller hit-and-run attacks. And twelve U.S. Army soldiers were missing.

A choked-up Marine was talking to his wife on my satellite phone, whispering, "I love you," when suddenly heavy gunfire and tracer rounds exploded in the distance. Helicopters roared overhead. What we didn't know then was that the rescue operation for nineteen-year-old Private First Class Jessica Lynch, one of the missing soldiers, had begun.

Navy SEALs and Army Rangers, acting on a tip from local Iraqis, swooped down on Nasiriya's Saddam Hospital prepared for enemy contact, only to discover Lynch's captors had fled. They found her in a bed on the third floor and whisked her to safety. Soon after, the remains of 11 bodies were discovered in shallow graves outside the hospital and feared to be Lynch's fellow soldiers.

The morning after the rescue, Marines escorted me to the hospital. There I met an Iraqi pharmacist named Imad, a short, round balding man with a mustache, wearing a white lab coat. Imad told me that he comforted Lynch during her "stay." He said, "Jessica cried every day for her family. . . . She was very happy when the Americans came." When I asked Imad how Jessica got there, and what he knew about the dead bodies, he looked away. "I don't know anything," he said, suddenly nervous.

Were those responsible somewhere nearby? Was I in their midst? All around me curious Iraqis were exchanging pleasantries with the Marines.

MIKE KIRSCH
REPORTER, WFOR/CBS NEWS

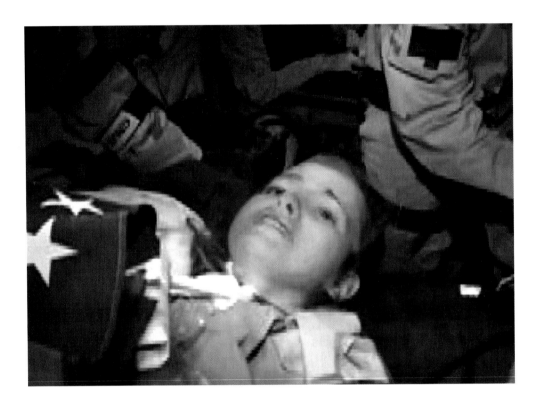

RESCUED

ABOVE Jessica Lynch was among the members of the Army's 507th Maintenance Company who were ambushed near Nasiriya on March 23, 2003. She was rescued from an Iraqi hospital on April 1, 2003, leading to celebrations in her hometown of Palestine, West Virginia.

OPPOSITE Lynch's mother embraces an Air National Guard major after news of her daughter's rescue.

ALL

BUTWON

CLOSING IN

After eight days in the desert, it was time for the First Brigade of the Third Infantry Division to push through the Karbala Gap and on toward Baghdad. On April 2, as they approached a bridge crossing the Euphrates River, the convoy encountered perhaps its stiffest resistance. To me and my crew, who had been embedded with the brigade ever since they'd entered Iraq from Kuwait thirteen days earlier, it seemed as if the Iraqis knew that once the U.S. Army crossed the bridge, the game was over. Next stop Baghdad. The resistance had all the feel of a last stand.

U.S. Army Apache helicopters slid in and out of the palm trees, popping up to shoot at Iraqis who were firing artillery and launching mortars at U.S. tanks and armored vehicles as they crossed the bridge. Clouds of smoke billowed skyward whenever an Apache or a Bradley found its target.

A few hours into the fighting, it was our turn to cross the bridge. A sergeant told us to drive as fast as we could and hope the Iraqis couldn't hit a moving target. The strategy seemed to work fine until about halfway across. That's when our Humvee just quit. Turning the key yielded only the sickening clicks of a starter attached to a dead engine. I could hear the whistling of AK-47 bullets flying overhead as the Iraqis took their shots at us.

I remember having enough time to think "We're in real trouble" when I felt a jolt. It was our colleagues at ABC News. They saw what was going on and positioned their truck right behind us. They hit the gas, latched on to our rear bumper, and pushed us to safety.

Everyone made it across the bridge that day. The First Brigade rested for a night, and the next day began the push to Saddam International Airport on the southwest outskirts of Baghdad. Up to that point, the war had been characterized by what had *not* happened: No chemical weapons, no armies of Islamic suicide bombers, no gas attacks. Had it all been too easy? The men in the First Brigade were nervous wondering whether the enemy had backed up into Baghdad, saving the worst for last.

Turns out they had little to worry about. The First Brigade met only pesky, occasional gunfire as they took the airport. The airport buildings—hangars, lounges, concourses—were empty. Triumph was in the air. But much more so was relief.

JIM AXELROD
CORRESPONDENT, CBS NEWS

ABOVE U.S. Army soldiers take cover behind
a Bradley fighting vehicle.

OPPOSITE Soldiers search buildings at an Iraqi
military compound south of Baghdad.

OVEALEAF U.S. Marines secure an Iraqi army
outpost and trading center near Numaniya.

ABOVE As U.S. forces closed in on Baghdad, Iraqi television showed Saddam Hussein walking through the streets of the capital.

LEFT Iraqi Information Minister Mohammed Saeed al-Sahhaf continued his defense of the regime. Saeed's absurd insistence on Iraqi victory earned him the nickname "Comical Ali" from reporters who attended his press conferences.

OPPOSITE As it turned out, protective gear for use in a chemical attack was not needed in Iraq.

U.S. Marines take positions during combat with Iraqi gunmen to secure a key bridge into Baghdad on April 6, 2003.

ABOVE U.S. Marines carry a wounded soldier to a casualty evacuation helicopter.

LEFT Near Baghdad, two Marines carry an injured Iraqi from his burning vehicle after he drove into a battle zone.

OPPOSITE A Marine tends to a comrade in shock after an attack.

DEAD WRONG

The charred, twisted remains of SUVs, some with "TV" visible on the side, gouts of congealing blood, and bits of clothing were strewn over several hundred square yards of a road junction about thirty miles from Mosul in northern Iraq. An hour earlier, out of a clear blue sky, a U.S. air strike, called in against Iraqi tanks by an Army officer, had instead hit a convoy of journalists and U.S.-backed Kurdish fighters. At least seventeen people died, among them a translator working for the BBC. Forty-five people were injured. It was the deadliest friendly fire incident of the war.

Rushing to the scene, my crew and I were stopped at a Kurdish checkpoint about a mile from the wreckage. "Why did you bomb us?" a Kurdish guerrilla lashed out. "You killed my friend." It was the first time in northern Iraq that identifying ourselves as being with American television had brought anything but smiles of welcome.

But his was a rare emotional outburst.

U.S. Special Forces positioned half a mile away from where the attack took place had no reaction, saying only that they'd been involved in "other issues" at the time. Kurdish guerrillas working with them seemed impressed by the firepower, but otherwise unfazed.

The Kurds' fierce sense of independence, coupled with a history of betrayal at the hands of more powerful nations, is summed up in an adage they repeat almost with pride, that Kurds "have no friends but the mountains." Accident though it was, one couldn't help but think that the friendly fire may have reinforced that belief.

ALLEN PIZZEY
CORRESPONDENT, CBS NEWS

In the worst friendly fire incident of the war, U.S. warplanes mistakenly bombed a convoy of U.S.-backed Kurdish fighters in northern Iraq on April 6, 2003.

MOURNING
U.S. troops grieve for fellow soldiers
killed during the war.

SACRIFICE

Her hands shaking and her voice weak, Amanda Jordan was exhausted, but determined to tell me her husband's story. She wanted the world to appreciate her husband's sacrifice.

On March 23, 2003, U.S. Marine Sergeant Phillip Jordan was one of a group of U.S. soldiers killed in an ambush at Nasiriya in which Iraqi fighters, who were dressed in civilian clothes and waving white flags of surrender, had opened fire.

Now, just days before his April 2 funeral, Amanda was getting ready to bury her husband. She and Phil had recently celebrated their ninth wedding anniversary—long distance. A card and a gift from Iraq arrived a few days after his death. But what overwhelmed her most was the thought of trying to gently help their six-year-old son Tyler understand that his father was gone. At one point, Tyler had asked his mother if he could telephone his daddy in heaven.

At the cemetery, Tyler had no choice but to understand. He sat with his mother, facing his father's flag-draped coffin. They looked so alone. When it came time to bury Phil Jordan, the flag was folded into its signature triangular shape, and a Marine officer walked over to Tyler and bent down on one knee. He spoke quietly to Tyler and then handed him the flag. And at that moment, like his mother beside him, Tyler wept.

MIKA BRZEZINSKI
CORRESPONDENT, CBS NEWS

GOOD-BYES

Back home, families and communities mourned the loss of loved ones.

FIGHTING CONTINUES IN IRAQ

On April 7, 2003, a U.S. warplane drops massive bombs on a site in an upscale Baghdad neighborhood where intelligence sources say Saddam Hussein was meeting with his sons.

WITNESS TO THE FALL

t was the last days of the regime that had ruled Iraq for more than three decades, but for those of us in Baghdad, it was never clear when the final moment would come.

Night after night my fellow journalists and I, who were staying at the Palestine Hotel in the center of the capital, were awakened an hour or so before sunrise by the distant roar of shells exploding and the crack of automatic weapons. Then on April 8, the battle came to our doorstep. A few hundred yards away, just across the Tigris River, the sky erupted in flames and smoke as U.S. troops fought for control of Saddam Hussein's main presidential palace. All that morning the air had been filled with the metallic scream of the U.S. Air Force's A-10 Warthogs as their heavy machine guns ripped into targets in downtown Baghdad.

That was also the day that a round from an American tank smashed into the Reuters television office on the hotel's fifteenth floor. Shattered concrete rained down on me and my Iraqi driver as we dove for cover on the second-floor balcony of the hotel. According to the U.S. Defense Department, the U.S. tank commander was returning fire. But none of the hundred or so journalists who witnessed what happened heard a single shot coming from the Palestine.

I lost someone I cared about that day, Reuters cameraman Taras Protsyuk, who died at the scene in spite of all efforts to save him. Spanish cameraman José Couso from Telecinco died a few hours later while undergoing surgery.

The next day, just before four P.M. local time, U.S. tanks rolled unopposed into the heart of Baghdad. They rumbled down the city's main commercial street to Firdos Square, right in front of the Palestine Hotel, without so much as a whisper from the elite Special Republican Guard

On April 8, 2003, a U.S. tank shelled Baghdad's Palestine Hotel, where journalists were staying, killing two cameramen.

or any of Iraq's other fighting forces. The Iraqi leadership had vanished.

As U.S. Marines warily assumed positions around the square, Iraqis began to emerge from nearby buildings, crying for revenge against Saddam Hussein. A man in the crowd grabbed my arm and shouted, "This finally is justice."

The world watched as Saddam Hussein's giant statue was torn from its platform by a U.S. tank and toppled to the ground. It disappeared in a frenzy of stomping feet as people swarmed over the broken torso, and U.S. Marines basked in the welcome that seemed to make their sacrifices worthwhile.

But Baghdad was not fully under American control, and no one was more aware of that than the Marines. They knew that the most dangerous time of all was just beginning. Even among those Iraqis who were grateful to be liberated, I could not find anyone who wanted the Americans to stay.

LARA LOGAN
CORRESPONDENT, CBS NEWS

U.S. Marines topple a giant statue of Saddam Hussein in central Baghdad on April 9, 2003.

DAY OF CONTRASTS
On April 9, 2003, U.S. troops are welcomed in some parts of Baghdad while fighting persisted in other sections of the city.

Grace Under Fire

t was the longest two hours of my life.

On April 9, while some U.S. Marines were toppling a forty-foot statue of Saddam Hussein in central Baghdad, I was about two miles away, in East Baghdad, with twenty-two Marines from Lima Company. Their mission was to secure the Iraqi Oil Ministry, a thirteen-story government building.

A few other squads joined us at the building; so altogether, about 80 Marines were there to get the job done. They broke into the back of the building, which turned out to be empty, except for a few looters carting away what little remained of office equipment and furniture.

In the meantime, about 200 Iraqi civilians—mostly men and a few children—had gathered just outside the eight-foot high wall that surrounds the ministry and were tearing down a life-size statue of Saddam. A party atmosphere prevailed. About a third of the Marines went out to watch the reveling around the fallen statue, another third were lounging on the steps of the building, and the rest were inside, enjoying a rare respite: The building was air conditioned. "I think this AC is our reward for making it to Baghdad," said one Marine. "You know, like the contestant on *Survivor* who gets a reward when he completes a challenge."

Moments later, the sharp, stuttering clack of an AK-47 sent the civilians rushing home and the Marines into defensive positions, either inside the building or up against the inside of the wall. My cameraman and I went to the wall with Lima Company's commander, Captain George Schreffler III, thirty-one, and seven of his men.

For the next hour or so, the gunfire grew louder and closer, punctuated every few moments by the explosive sound of rocket-propelled grenades. But the Marines hardly returned any fire. I saw no fear, no confusion among the Marines. In the three weeks en route to Baghdad, they had been shot at a lot. At first they had responded to any provocation with a barrage. But as time went on, they learned that if they held their fire, the assailants usually just went away or ran out of bullets.

So for nearly an hour, the Marines used their heads, not their weapons, trying to figure out where the fire was coming from—the enemy was clearly moving around and the incoming fire was from different directions—and waiting for the opportunity to shoot to kill.

At one point during the attack, a corporal who had been on one of the building's higher floors ran to Captain Schreffler, breathlessly explaining that he'd "eyeballed" at least one of the gunmen and asking for permission to shoot. Schreffler, who was sitting on the ground with his ankles crossed, relaxed like a guy gone fishing, listened politely as gunfire crackled over our heads. Then he asked, "Have you positively identified the weapon?"

The corporal responded with various details: the fire was coming from a nearby white apartment building, also surrounded by a wall; he had seen three heads popping up and down from behind the wall; the plaster that fell off the ministry building when it was hit further confirmed where the fire was coming from.

"Have you seen the weapon?" Schreffler asked.

The answer was no.

"Do not take the shot," Schreffler said.

The corporal was disappointed. And truth be told, so was I and from what I could sense, so were the men within earshot of the conversation. We were being peppered with gunfire and blasted by grenades; cement rained down on us whenever the building was hit. The urge to shoot back was strong.

Our attention was riveted on the apartment building the corporal had pinpointed. About fifteen minutes later, we all saw them: three heads, moving slowly along the wall, until they emerged from behind it into the street—a man, a woman, and a little girl, obviously a family.

Not long after that, two snipers were positively identified and killed in a wave of U.S. fire. There were probably more shooters, but they didn't respond to the U.S. show of force. Everything went quiet, and remained so.

Weeks later, when I was back in the United States, I called Captain Schreffler's father. I had promised to send him a copy of the video that had been made that day and I wanted to make sure he had received it.

"I'm so proud of that kid," said his father, George Schreffler, Jr. I choked back tears, remembering that his son had saved innocent civilians that day. I was proud of him too.

BYRON PITTS
CORRESPONDENT, CBS NEWS

CONTACT
Patrolling Baghdad neighborhoods, U.S. forces interact with Iraqi civilians.

TAKING IT
DAY BY DAY

On April 9, I spoke with soldiers from the Second Platoon of Bravo Company, Eleventh Engineer Battalion in south central Baghdad. They'd set up camp alongside a road, and they were shaving, brushing their teeth, getting their hair cut, soaking their feet, and doing laundry. They were obviously trying to get rid of the nearly three weeks' worth of dirt, grime, and sweat they had accumulated since the war had started.

Most of the other U.S. troops in Baghdad were relieved, if not happy, about the fall of Baghdad. But among the soldiers in the Second Platoon, the mood was somber.

In securing Saddam International Airport southwest of Baghdad, soldiers in the Second Platoon had come under fire. And in the days after moving into the city, they had been the targets of intermittent attacks.

But that had not been the worst of it: In the previous five days, Second Platoon had lost two sergeants in combat, and was now under the leadership of a third sergeant in the chain of command.

Their first leader, thirty-three-year-old Sergeant First Class Paul R. Smith, had been killed outside Baghdad on April 4. He had jumped into an armored personnel carrier when his unit came under attack. Smith had taken control of the .50-caliber machine gun mounted on top of the carrier. He fired about 200 shots, providing cover for twenty soldiers before he was hit by incoming fire.

The job of rallying the young soldiers fell to Staff Sergeant Lincoln Hollinsaid, twenty-seven. But he didn't get much of a chance. Three days later, Hollinsaid was killed in a grenade attack in Baghdad.

Now Second Platoon was seeking solace in the routines of daily life. "That kind of stuff does happen in war," said Private Michael Seaman, "but it's not supposed to happen to us."

JIM AXELROD
CORRESPONDENT, CBS NEWS

AFTERMATH
U.S. military continued to patrol
Baghdad after the collapse of
the regime.

LAWLESSNESS AND DISORDER

t was April 14, and another day of heat and sandy haze was ending. The Marines we were with had assumed a defensive position about 300 yards from the Tigris along a short stretch of the main thoroughfare, Abu Nawas Street. But there was no traffic. The city was paralyzed by fear, chaos, and anarchy. The fall of Baghdad had left the capital a looter's paradise.

In the last twenty-four hours, one Marine from another unit had been shot and killed by two men who approached him at a checkpoint. The day before that, a man strapped with explosives had blown himself up at another checkpoint, wounding four Marines and a medical corpsman, two critically.

The Marines along the riverbank knew all about those bloody actions. They spoke of them little, but you knew such actions were on their minds as they scanned the street and riverbank in silence.

A waxing moon was becoming visible at their backs. Across the river was the 14th of Ramadan Mosque, one of Baghdad's landmarks, and Arabic calls to prayer echoed across the river water from the building's loudspeakers.

Suddenly, from the direction of the river's near edge, came the unmistakable "pop-pop." Everyone stiffened. A tank turret turned toward the sound, and the .50-caliber on an armored vehicle swiveled and aimed. But the Marines did not fire.

There was another, longer, more sustained burst of incoming. This time the Marines responded. Twenty minutes of hellish gunfire followed. The tank's cannon rumbled, interspersed with rocket-propelled grenade explosions and rifle pops.

This was urban combat—ugly, confusing, and lethal. In this case, the attackers' original fire apparently came from a small building. The building was hit repeatedly, but no bodies were found. No one was wounded or captured.

How many attackers there were and who they were is unknown. What we do know is that this kind of skirmishing went on from time to time in various sections of what the Marines called "Bad City."

By any reasonable analysis, one of the points inherent in these experiences was this: the U.S. military commanded Baghdad and its environs, but it did not yet completely control them. The American force involved was thin, and the work being demanded by Washington was increasing.

Besides engaging in urban combat and fighting in the city's outskirts;

besides being a protective force for key bridges, streets, hotels, and hospitals; and besides protecting their own units, soldiers were taking on rapidly expanding duties in restarting and administering a wide variety of city services. In some cases, they were being asked to serve as social workers.

Call it peacekeeping if you like, but by whatever name, it was a heavy load for a light force.

DAN RATHER
CORRESPONDENT, CBS NEWS

INJURED CIVILIANS

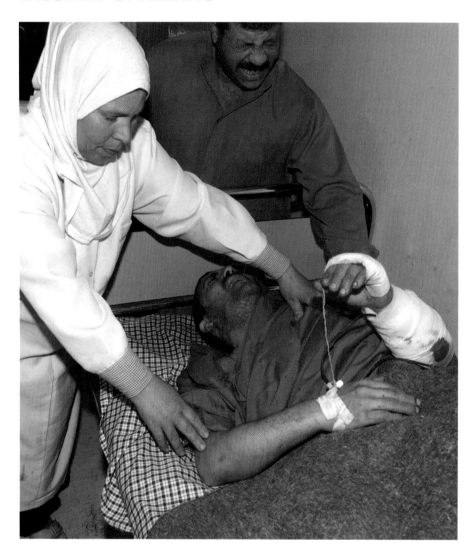

CAUGHT IN THE CROSS FIRE

n one of Baghdad's main hospitals, I stumbled across a fifteen-year-old boy lying on a stretcher next to the elevator. He was one of about a dozen patients who were crammed into the suffocating hallway waiting for surgery. His distorted limbs, wrapped in blood-soaked bandages, were waiting to be amputated as he slipped in and out of consciousness.

"Cluster bomb," the surgeon said to me, looking at the boy, and shrugged his soldiers.

It was just over a week after Baghdad had fallen to U.S. forces, and the heavy fighting was over, but the killing continued. Looting and lawlessness had taken hold of the city.

A twelve-year-old Iraqi girl had been lying in the hospital for days. Her small head was covered with gauze because of a bullet lodged in her skull. She had been shot by Iraqi looters when she left home to fetch water for her family in a suburb of Baghdad: Another victim of the random gunfire that quickly replaced the echo of bombs in the streets of the capital as criminal elements flooded into the power vacuum left by Saddam Hussein's regime.

As I walked through the hospital, a man stopped me. He held up a framed photograph of his nine-month-old baby and in broken English told me how her face had burned when an American tank hit their car. As he spoke, he gestured to the two short stumps of thigh that were all that remained of the legs he lost in that explosion. He was not the only one. In the next room lay a mother with only one leg, and near her, another man with no legs.

This is what the Pentagon calls "collateral damage," and it is inevitable in war, no matter how smart your weapons. But try telling that to the victims who asked me over and over again: "Where is George Bush? He promised he would make our lives better and we believed him. Where is he? Tell him we are waiting, please . . . tell him."

LARA LOGAN
CORRESPONDENT, CBS NEWS

LEFT **After days of anarchy, U.S. Marines began to arrest suspected looters in Baghdad.**

ABOVE **An Iraqi man surveys the vault of the National Museum of Antiquities after looters damaged and stole priceless artifacts.**

RIGHT **Lawlessness was not confined to Baghdad: On April 10, 2003, a prominent pro-Western cleric was murdered at this shrine in the holy city of Najaf.**

THE ACCIDENTAL MAYOR

A four-lane concrete bridge vaults over the Tigris River at a town called Numaniya, southeast of Baghdad. The bridge was a vital link for U.S. and British armor, and it was the job of Lieutenant Colonel Brent Dunahoe to keep it open. But to do so, Dunahoe soon discovered, he would also have to govern 40,000 anxious, angry Iraqis whose war-torn mud-brick town was without water, electricity, or the rule of law. So by mid-April, as the major combat phase of the war drew to an end, Dunahoe set out to reestablish order and basic services. A no-nonsense Texan, he became the accidental mayor of Numaniya.

"Do you have a police force in this town?" I asked.

"Yes. The United States Marine Corps," Dunahoe growled. "We're controlling the town."

Despite Dunahoe's swagger, Numaniya remained stubbornly out of control. Dunahoe's engineers didn't have the parts needed to restore power. His doctors manned a hospital virtually without medicine. When Dunahoe held his first town meeting with village elders on April 16, the townspeople brought a few of their sick and wounded to the meeting hall and laid them on the sidewalk in a desperate plea for help. "What do they think I can do?" Dunahoe whispered to an aide. "Heal the sick?"

To subdue the street, Dunahoe established a 10 P.M. curfew. One night my cameraman and I walked on a foot patrol led by Sergeant Levi Pfeiffer, a twenty-two-year-old from Pottstown, Pennsylvania. "After curfew, we try to shoo them into their houses," he said. "If we get any kind of resistance, we 'cuff and stuff.' We cuff their hands and pull a bag over their heads and detain them for a few hours." Then, without irony, he added, "We're just trying to show them what freedom is like."

Many residents in town were already grumbling about the "freedom" the invasion had brought. I asked a schoolteacher, Keh Hamil, how he felt about being free after thirty-five years. "Am I?" he asked. "Or have we traded one regime for another?"

Lieutenant Colonel Dunahoe couldn't say just when the village should expect power or water or even the reopening of schools. But at the town meeting, he did suggest his own timetable. "My intent is to help you secure a happy future and then to return to the United States in time for football season—*American* football season—so I can watch my son play."

It was one commander's hope that the residents would be on their own in only six months. It seemed an optimistic goal, even for a small river town.

SCOTT PELLEY
CORRESPONDENT, CBS NEWS

LEFT General Tommy Franks and his top military commanders meet with reporters in one of Saddam Hussein's Baghdad palaces on April 16, 2003. Franks tells the journalists that the combat phase of the war is over.

ABOVE U.S. Marines secure Tikrit, Saddam Hussein's hometown and a stronghold of his Baathist Party.

GOING HOME

RIGHT **U.S. POWs, who were found after the fall of Baghdad, begin the first leg of their journey back to the United States.**

OPPOSITE **A few lucky troops returned to the United States shortly after the collapse of the Iraqi regime, though most remained in Iraq. Here, a sailor, who served on the USS *Abraham Lincoln* is reunited with her ten-month-old son in San Diego.**

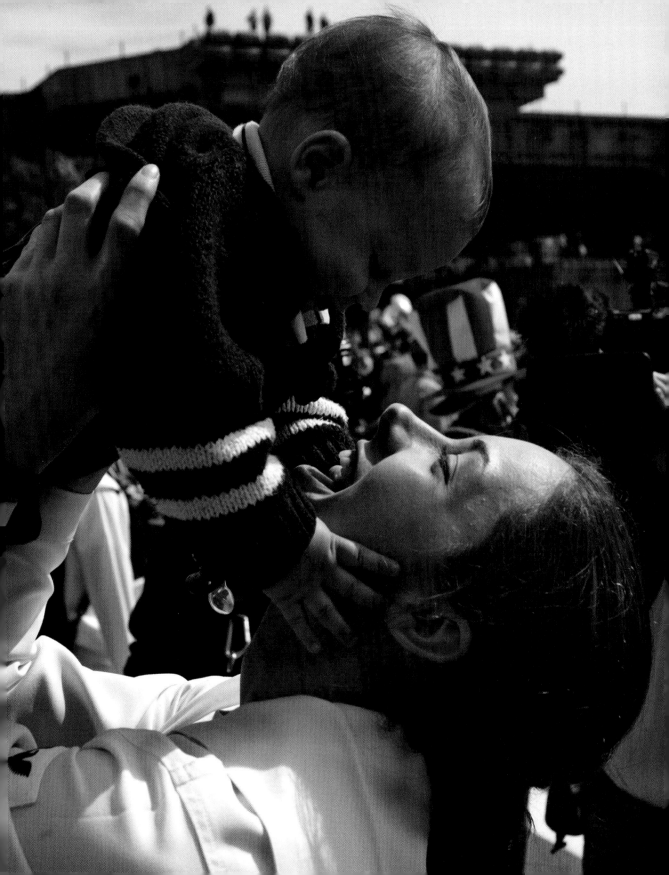

AFTERWORD

've lost track of how many times I've driven the road to Baghdad from Amman, Jordan, but I've been doing it for more than twenty years. On an early morning in June 2003, six weeks after leaving Iraq shortly following the war, I was back on that same road. On each of my earlier trips—during the 1980s Iran-Iraq war, after the 1991 Gulf War, and in the frequent times of tension since then—Iraq has seemed to reveal less of itself with each journey.

This time the highway seemed to lead directly into the rising, eye-searing sun, and I squinted into a world of dark silhouettes and shadows. It was a metaphoric vision of Iraq's eternal mystery, which I had always blamed on the pathological secrecy of Saddam Hussein's Baathist regime. But now with Saddam Hussein gone and Iraq's future no clearer, the place seemed even more difficult to fathom.

Nowhere was the confusion more obvious than in Falluja, about thirty miles west of Baghdad. The U.S. Army had moved into the town in force, to quell what military officials were calling "isolated" attacks by diehard Saddam loyalists, but which seemed to me and other observers like a nascent, organized resistance movement. The mere appearance of a television camera was enough to incite a riot. And on a day when there had been fifteen attacks on American troops across the country, one otherwise normal looking middle-aged man was actually spitting with rage as he screamed into the lens of the CBS camera: "Go!" he shouted, "We do not like Saddam. But we hate Americans. Leave this place!" He said that he felt more occupied than liberated, and he knew who to blame for all of Iraq's current woes—the United States.

It would be facile to say that winning the peace might prove more difficult than winning the war—facile, but probably true. The resentment to a U.S. presence that was expressed in Falluja was felt almost everywhere else I went. U.S. troops hadn't helped their cause in the early days after the war by responding to threatening crowds with volleys of machine-gun fire.

Moreover, what was missing was any sense of a coherent U.S. plan to rebuild the country. Already the man who was supposed to supervise the reconstruction, retired Army General Jay Garner, had been replaced by Paul Bremer, a career U.S. diplomat with—it was hoped—a more politically savvy touch. Yet one of Bremer's first moves was to abandon the previously announced plan for a national conference to choose an interim Iraqi administration because nobody could agree on who should be part of the effort.

All sorts of political groupings were jockeying for position and none of them, Bremer said, was representative enough to take even limited power. In a country where the only previous political structure, the Baathist Party, was now illegal, and where the very concept of opposition power bases had been literally beaten out of the population, there was no consensus on a path to the future. Formerly exiled, often antagonistic opposition groups were vying with emerging religious, ethnic, regional, and tribal interests. And everybody mistrusted everybody else.

Amid this gloom, though, there were some encouraging signs. Public political debate had begun. A range of new newspapers appeared; and although they were each aligned to one of the developing political groups and often full of unsubstantiated drivel, their very existence signaled a freedom of expression only dreamed of before. People devoured them. Satellite dishes also began sprouting on rooftops as Iraqis reached out to a world that all but a well-connected few had previously been denied.

One incident I witnessed hinted at the country's possibilities. As I rolled along in heavy traffic one day on a central Baghdad boulevard, the road dipped into a long underpass where everything screeched to a halt. The driver of a car about ten vehicles ahead had spotted that the road was blocked by a burst water main, and he raised his hand. So did the drivers behind him. And without anyone saying a word, three lanes of vehicles backed up out of the underpass in unison, while the traffic behind us waited. Everyone then filed in orderly fashion onto a side road.

This was common action for the common good. This was patience and the unspoken acknowledgment that unless everyone moved together, no one would move at all. This was, for the Iraqis themselves and for the men and women who had fought this war to make Iraq a better, less threatening place, a cause for hope.

MARK PHILLIPS
CORRESPONDENT, CBS NEWS